Steps to Breakthrough

Freedom from Life's Hurts

Crosspointe Ministries
www.sueboldt.com

For more information about having a

Steps to Breakthrough

conference for your church, women's event, or retreat, please contact *Sue Boldt* at sueboldt.com
or
susanboldt@gmail.com

Cover Photo: Brittney Borowski
Lightstock.com

Steps to Breakthrough

Table of Contents

Introduction

"The Spirit of the Lord GOD is upon Me
Because the LORD has anointed Me
To preach good tidings to the poor;
He has sent Me to heal the brokenhearted,
To proclaim liberty to the captives,
And the opening of the prison to those who are bound;"
Isaiah 61:1

Dear Loved One,

One thing we have learned for certain from God's Word...

The Lord Jesus wants His children to be whole, well, and flourishing. It is His heart that each one of us experiences His inexhaustible love no matter what life is currently throwing our direction. The Scriptures declare this truth over and over again regardless of our past hurts, our present realities, or our future concerns.

That you may really come to know
practically, through experience for yourselves
the love of Christ, which far surpasses
mere knowledge without experience;
that you may be filled through all your being
unto all the fullness of God,
may have the richest measure of the divine Presence,
and become a body wholly filled and flooded with God Himself!
Ephesians 3:19-20 AMPC

It is our prayer that this *Steps to Breakthrough Workbook* will be used by the Lord Jesus as a tool for you to take a *step* forward to finding greater freedom in your personal life. Along with those ministering to you today, we pray you will discover Biblical tools to release you from the chains and knots of your past to propel you into all He has for you now and for your future. Then, in turn, we are requesting that you will also know the rich fulfillment of helping others find greater freedom from life's hurts for themselves.

Jesus has brought you here to this moment. He will not disappoint. Those presenting this Biblical approach to freedom today both love you and they have been ardently praying for you. Together, we cheer you on in this journey to breakthrough for all God has in store for your life.

"The thief does not come except to steal, and to kill, and to destroy.
I have come that they may have life, and that they may have it more abundantly."
John 10:10

Hearing God's Voice

"But He who enters by the door is the shepherd of the sheep.

To Him the doorkeeper opens, and the sheep hear His voice; and He calls his own sheep by name and leads them out.

And when He brings out his own sheep, He goes before them; and the sheep follow Him, for they know His voice.

Yet they will by no means follow a stranger, but will flee from him, for they do not know the voice of strangers."

... Then Jesus said to them again, "Most assuredly, I say to you, I am the door of the sheep.

All who ever came before Me are thieves and robbers, but the sheep did not hear them.

I am the door. If anyone enters by Me, he will be saved, and will go in and out and find pasture.

The thief does not come except to steal, and to kill, and to destroy.

I have come that they may have life, and that they may have it more abundantly.

I am the good shepherd. The good shepherd gives His life for the sheep.

The hireling flees because he is a hireling and does not care about the sheep.

I am the good shepherd; and I know My sheep, and am known by My own."

John 10:2-5, 7-11, 13-14

What is Jesus Saying to me?

You are my refuge and my shield;
your word is my source of hope.
Psalm 119:114 NLT

But Jesus answered him, saying,
"It is written, man shall not live by bread alone,
but by every word of God."
Luke 4:4

Hearing God's Voice

I am the true vine, and My Father is the vinedresser.

Every branch in Me that does not bear fruit He takes away; and every branch that bears fruit He prunes, that it may bear more fruit.

You are already clean because of the word which I have spoken to you.

Abide in Me, and I in you. As the branch cannot bear fruit of itself, unless it abides in the vine, neither can you, unless you abide in Me.

I am the vine, you are the branches. He who abides in Me, and I in him, bears much fruit;

for without Me you can do nothing.

If you abide in Me, and My words abide in you, you will ask what you desire, and it shall be done for you.

By this My Father is glorified, that you bear much fruit; so you will be My disciples.

As the Father loved Me, I also have loved you; abide in My love.

If you keep My commandments, you will abide in My love, just as I have kept My Father's commandments and abide in His love.

These things I have spoken to you, that My joy may remain in you, and that your joy may be full.

You did not choose Me, but I chose you and appointed you that you should go and bear fruit, and

that your fruit should remain, that whatever you ask the Father in My name He may give you.

John 15:1-5, 7-11, 16

What is Jesus Saying to me?

And take the helmet of salvation,
and the sword of the Spirit, which is the word of God.
Ephesians 6:17

Then Jesus said to those Jews who believed Him,
"If you abide in My word, you are My disciples indeed.
And you shall know the truth,
and the truth shall make you free."
John 8:31-32

Hearing God's Voice

Therefore I say to you, do not worry about your life, what you will eat or what you will drink;

nor about your body, what you will put on.

Is not life more than food and the body more than clothing?

Look at the birds of the air, for they neither sow nor reap nor gather into barns; yet your heavenly Father feeds them. Are you not of more value than they?

Which of you by worrying can add one cubit to his stature? So why do you worry about clothing?

Consider the lilies of the field, how they grow: they neither toil nor spin; and yet I say to you that

even Solomon in all his glory was not arrayed like one of these.

Now if God so clothes the grass of the field, which today is, and tomorrow is thrown into the oven,

will He not much more clothe you, O you of little faith? "Therefore do not worry, saying, 'What

shall we eat?' or 'What shall we drink?' or 'What shall we wear?

For after all these things the Gentiles seek. For your heavenly Father knows that you need all these things.

But seek first the kingdom of God and His righteousness, and all these things shall be added to you.

Therefore do not worry about tomorrow, for tomorrow will worry about its own things.

Sufficient for the day is its own trouble.

Matthew 6:25-34

What is Jesus Saying to me?

Sanctify them by Your truth.
Your word is truth.
John 17:17

Your word is a lamp to my feet
And a light to my path.
Psalm 119:105

Hearing God's Voice

May He grant you out of the rich treasury of His glory to be strengthened *and* reinforced with

mighty power in the inner man by the Holy Spirit Himself indwelling your innermost being and personality.

May Christ through your faith actually dwell, settle down, abide, make His permanent home

in your hearts! May you be rooted deep in love *and* founded securely on love,

That you may have the power *and* be strong to apprehend *and* grasp with all the saints, God's de-

voted people, the experience of that love what is the breadth and length and height and depth of it;

That you may really come to know, practically, through experience for yourselves, the love of

Christ, which far surpasses mere knowledge without experience; that you may be filled through

all your being unto all the fullness of God [may have the richest measure of the divine Presence,

and become a body wholly filled and flooded with God Himself]!

Now to Him Who, by in consequence of the action of His power that is at work within us, is

able to carry out His purpose and do superabundantly, far over *and* above all that we dare ask or

think [infinitely beyond our highest prayers, desires, thoughts, hopes, or dreams]—

To Him be glory in the church and in Christ Jesus throughout all generations forever and ever. Amen so be it.

Ephesians 3:16-21 AMPC (Most parentheses and brackets removed for easier reading)

What is Jesus Saying to me?

If you abide in Me, and My words abide in you,
you will ask what you desire, and it shall be done for you.
John 15:7

He sent His word and healed them,
And delivered them from their destructions.
Psalm 107:20

Hearing God's Voice

So you have not received a spirit that makes you fearful slaves. Instead, you received God's Spirit

when he adopted you as his own children. Now we call him, "Abba, Father." For his Spirit joins with

our spirit to affirm that we are God's children. And since we are his children, we are his heirs. In fact, together with Christ we are heirs of God's glory.

But if we are to share his glory, we must also share his suffering. ...

And we know that God causes everything to work together for the good of those who love God and are called according to his purpose for them.

... What shall we say about such wonderful things as these? If God is for us, who can ever be against

us? Since he did not spare even his own Son but gave him up for us all, won't he also give us everything else? ...

Can anything ever separate us from Christ's love? Does it mean he no longer loves us if we have

trouble or calamity, or are persecuted, or hungry, or destitute, or in danger, or threatened with death?

... No, despite all these things, overwhelming victory is ours through Christ, who loved us. And I am

convinced that nothing can ever separate us from God's love. Neither death nor life, neither angels

nor demons, neither our fears for today nor our worries about tomorrow--not even the powers of hell

can separate us from God's love. No power in the sky above or in the earth below--indeed, nothing in

all creation will ever be able to separate us from the love of God that is revealed in Christ Jesus our

Lord."   *Romans 8:15-17, 28, 31-32, 35, 37-39 NLT*

What is Jesus Saying to me?

So shall My word be that goes forth from My mouth;
It shall not return to Me void,
But it shall accomplish what I please,
And it shall prosper in the thing for which I sent it.
Isaiah 55:11

Knowing Him in the Secret Place

He who dwells in the secret place of the Most High Shall
abide under the shadow of the Almighty.
Psalm 91:1

But you, when you pray, go into your room,
and when you have shut your door,
pray to your Father who is in the secret place;
and your Father who sees in secret will reward you openly.
Matthew 6:6

You prepare a feast for me
in the presence of my enemies.
You honor me by anointing my head with oil.
My cup overflows with blessings.
Psalm 23:5 NLT

Knowing Him in the Secret Place

You will show me the path of life;
In Your presence is fullness of joy;
At Your right hand are pleasures forevermore.
Psalm 16:11

One thing have I asked of the Lord, that will I seek, inquire
for, and insistently require:
that I may dwell in the house of the Lord, in His presence,
all the days of my life,
to behold and gaze upon the beauty
[the sweet attractiveness and the delightful loveliness]
of the Lord
and to meditate, consider, and inquire in His temple.
Psalm 27:4 AMPC

Who We Are

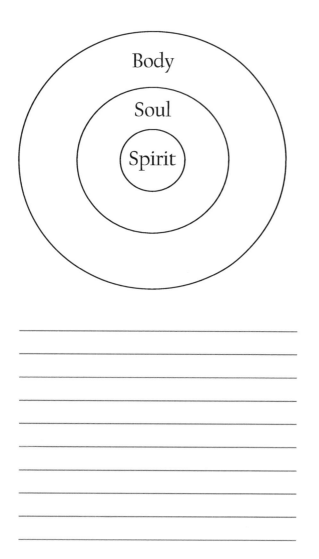

Spirit

Pneuma (Greek). Compare with pneumonia, pneumatic. Breath, breeze, a current of air, wind, spirit. The unseen part of a person that was rendered lifeless until the point of receiving Christ *Romans 5:12, Ephesians 2:2-4, John 3:3-8.* The place within a person where communion with God is possible by the complete indwelling of the Holy Spirit *John 7:37-39, Romans 8:9-11.*

Soul

Psyche (Greek). Compare psychology, psychiatry. The seat of emotions (heart), thoughts (mind), intellect, conscience, ability to reason, desires, the ability to make decisions, and the unique, one-of-a-kind personality given to each of us.

Body

Soma (Greek). The living, physical human body. The external person with five senses: taste, touch, sight, hearing, smell, and taste. The intricate, breathing, and living creation of God *Psalm 139:13-14,* to house the soul and spirit.

_____

_____

_____

_____

_____

_____

_____

_____

_____

The Power of the Holy Spirit

"...Jesus stood and cried out, saying,
"If anyone thirsts, let him come to Me and drink.
He who believes in Me, as the Scripture has said,
out of his heart will flow rivers of living water."
But this He spoke concerning the Spirit,
whom those believing in Him would receive..."
John 7:37-39

"If a son asks for bread from any father among you,
will he give him a stone? Or if he asks for a fish,
will he give him a serpent instead of a fish...? "
"If you then, being evil, know how to give good gifts to your children,
how much more will your heavenly Father
give the Holy Spirit to those who ask Him!"
Luke 11:11-13

The Nature of Strongholds

"The Spirit of the Lord GOD is upon Me
Because the LORD has anointed Me
To preach good tidings to the poor;
He has sent Me to heal the brokenhearted,
To proclaim liberty to the captives,
And the opening of the prison to those who are bound;"
Isaiah 61:1   Luke 4:18

When we first came to faith in the saving grace of the Lord Jesus Christ, each of saw an immediate difference in our lives for the better.

Hope, joy, forgiveness! A fresh clean start! His love overwhelming our hearts! We knew we were being indescribably transformed from the inside-out; we were being irrevocably changed by the power of the gospel – or good news – of Jesus' rescue mission for us personally.

Nevertheless, perhaps a few years down the road on our journey with the Lord, we now seem to find ourselves in the same predicament Paul found himself in of *doing things he didn't want to do and not doing what he should.* Try as we might, we can't seem to resist or break free from thoughts, behaviors, or long held patterns of life that we know aren't glorifying to God.

We fall into an old, harmful habit or addiction
We feel remorse
We confess our sin
We experience tremendous guilt
We try to repent and we say we will do better
We then try harder and...
We fail again

A cycle of failure seems to repeat itself over and over again. What may be particularly disconcerting is when we have experienced a measure of freedom in a certain area of difficulty, but then a situation may occur that triggers old responses. Does this sound familiar?

Some of us may have deep pain in our hearts or debilitating fears which appear out of nowhere without a moment's notice. We can't seem to forgive certain people. Our tempers flare-up without warning. We may have a low-grade temperature, as it were, of shame, guilt, or disappointment about ourselves – or what the Bible calls a spirit of heaviness or depression.

Others of us may not be able to let go of a life circumstance – a death, divorce, the loss of health, a job, or a relationship. This keeps us from experiencing the abundant, excessive, over-flowing life Jesus talks about. Our spirits are intact, but our souls are like a city whose walls have broken down and our "enemies" – sinful and rampant thoughts, desires, and habits – have easy access to dominate us no matter how much we want or *will* it to be otherwise.

But, Jesus came...

God became flesh, to rescue us from behind enemy lines. Our belief in the One and Only Savior brought us back into fellowship with our loving Father for eternity. And that is not all Jesus did for us. He came to bring **breakthrough** from the slavery of our past into the freedom of His abundant life now. He came to *loosen us from the pain* of hurts, wounds, words, and circumstances which color the way we live, how we view ourselves, others, and even how we view God.

> *. . . For this purpose the Son of God was manifested,*
> *that He might **destroy** the works of the devil.*
> 1 John 3:8b

Let's take a closer look at the Greek New Testament definition of the word *destroy* from the verse we just read:

Lyo Meaning: *To loosen what is bound, to untie. To loose, let go, set free. To dissolve, sever, break, to destroy and demolish, to make void or dissolve.*

Make this scripture very personal to you. Jesus came to *destroy, untie,* and *demolish* your hurts, wounds, strongholds, and any lies you may be believing. He also came to do this for the people you love and are in the realm of your influence. Jesus came so we could be restored as His darling children, the beat of His heart. As His children He has given us His authority to take back the dominion that once was ours, but lost to the devil at Adam's fall.

> *Behold, I give you the authority to trample on serpents*
> *and scorpions, and over all the power of the enemy, and*
> *nothing shall by any means hurt you.*
> *Nevertheless do not rejoice in this, that the spirits are*
> *subject to you, but rather rejoice because your names*
> *are written in heaven.*
> Luke 10:19-20

Somewhere, sometime in the midst of Jesus' rescue mission for my heart and mind, He spoke very clearly to me, "*You believed a lie rather than My truth.*" The minute He said this to my heart, I knew it was so. I knew the Word of God, but a lie was quicker, easier, and more effortless to believe. Truth requires *faith* on our part. Lies simply require less effort and less day-in, day-out personal intimacy with God. Think of it this way: my believing a lie was equal to pulling the adversary's veil back over my soul. No more.

It is time for us to make the choice if we really believe the Word of God or not. It is time to start taking Jesus at His Word and engage in the skirmishes and battles the enemy is waging all around us; exercising the power of Jesus Name!

The Roaring Lion...

This enemy – who is not only full of darkness – is a ***liar***. Jesus, when speaking to the religious leaders who so vehemently opposed Him, said the following:

> *You are of your father the devil, and the desires of your father you want to do. He was murderer from the beginning, and does not stand in the truth, because **there is no truth in him**. When he speaks a **lie**, he speaks from his own resources, for **he is a liar and the father of it**.*
> John 8:44

Where does the adversary speak his lies? In our minds and through our thoughts.

Often when our souls have been wounded by our past experiences, that same serpent of old – by use of his demons – usually comes to present a lie to us. The enemy does not play fair. He truly is a roaring lion — toothless, yet wily and destructive — seeking whom he may devour as Peter tells us. He is very good at ensnaring us, especially in our early childhood up through puberty when we are most vulnerable, when we would not even begin to know how to resist a lie with truth. Again, is this fair? No! *Remember the devil is pure evil.* When we are at our weakest or are most defenseless, his words *seem to appear as the truth*, confirming what we may have experienced.

"There you go, you've messed up, AGAIN. You always do or
   say the wrong thing. Nobody could ever love you."
"That awful thing happened to you. You are not important.

You don't matter. God didn't see what happened."

"See, you were over-looked...again – you must not be worth someone's time. You do not have value."

"God's done it again. He has disappointed you.
He is not worth trusting."

"God answered that person's prayer, but not yours. He doesn't really love you."

"God is sure taking His time about this; maybe you had better take matters into your own hands. He has forgotten you."

The Apostle Paul gives us great warning and advice in one simple phrase:

> *"Be angry, and do not sin": do not let the sun go down on your wrath,*
> ***nor give place to the devil."***
> Eph 4:26-27

What is the original New Testament Greek meaning of this phrase? What does it mean to give the adversary a ***place***?

Topos – Meaning: English *"Topography."* A place, portion, ground, or a space marked off. A condition, position or station held by someone, such as in a company or assembly. An opportunity, power or occasion for acting.

Strongholds...

Much like in any war the world has seen where an enemy army has advanced and gained ground, that place has become an enemy *stronghold*. When we give place to the enemy's *lies* for any length of time, it's as if we have made an agreement that these lies *are* true. These lies can become *strongholds* in our soul for him to set up shop and torment us. Most of the time we won't even realize what has happened. He has gained *topography* in our hearts, minds, personality, or intellect, and we cannot free ourselves because these lies now have a *strong hold* on us. These are scratches in the record of our souls we talked about earlier that we just can't seem to get past.

In early childhood we are seldom equipped to recognize the enemy's advances and lies. Many of us were not raised in Christian homes or we grew up in Christian homes that had little knowledge of God's Word in regard to spiritual warfare. God sees everything. He stops *most* of what the enemy throws at us without us even knowing, yet we still live behind enemy lines. In our ignorance and human nature, we often find it is easier to believe the devil's lies rather than have faith in the truth of God's love for us.

What are these lies about?

Lies about you.
Lies about God.

We think if we just *try harder* we will have success over these strongholds in our lives. We often experience so much guilt when we fail time after time that we can hardly bear it. Our intentions to break free are good, but we don't have the power to do so without the truth of God's Word and the strength of the Holy Spirit. These strongholds are places where Satan has a territory of our *soul* that has brought *oppression* to our lives. We have made agreements with the enemy because we have believed his lies about ourselves and/or about God, rather than the truth of God's Word. (This is *not* possession by the enemy – he can't touch our spirits, the dwelling place of the Holy Spirit!)

If you think you may have areas of enemy oppression, don't despair. Instead think, "Yes, I do have some knots (don't we all!), but Jesus loves me so much and He is so powerful, these knots are easy for Him to untie. He won't stop until they are completely loosed and I am free!"

When Jesus cried, "It is finished!" on the cross, He completely destroyed the enemy. Victory and freedom are our inheritance in Christ and whom the Son sets free is free indeed!

It is amazing how the Scriptures bear this out. From Genesis to Revelation, God's Word repeatedly warns us about the lies of the enemy. As you read the Bible now, you will be amazed at the frequency of this recurring theme.

Pastor Christopher J. Hayward, the President of Cleansing Stream Ministries, succinctly states:

> *"Strongholds are first established in the mind; that is why we are to take every thought captive. Behind a stronghold is also a lie – a place of personal bondage where God's Word has been subjugated to any unscriptural idea or personally confused belief that is held to be true. Behind every lie is a fear, and behind every fear is an idol. Idols are established wherever there exists a failure to trust in the provisions of God that are ours through Jesus Christ."*

As we understand these spiritual principles we will find much of the Old Testament making more sense to us. Think of it. Israel's exodus out of Egypt and entrance to the Promised Land is a type of our own exodus out of the enemy's strongholds in our lives. Our freedom is our Promised Land...our inheritance in Christ. The rebuilding of Jerusalem's walls in the book of Nehemiah is a great study regarding the rebuilding of our broken and battered souls. Instance after instance in the Old Testament are pictures of God's working in our lives.

What God spoke to the Old Testament prophet Hosea applies directly to the devil when He was commanding judgment against the false or lying prophets of Israel:

> "'Therefore thus says the Lord GOD: "Behold, I am against your magic charms by which **you hunt souls there like birds**. I will tear them from your arms, and let the souls go, the souls you hunt like birds.
>
> I will also tear off your **veils** and **deliver My** people out of your hand, and they shall no longer be as prey in your hand. Then you shall know that I am the LORD.
>
> "Because with **lies** you have made the heart of the righteous sad, whom I have not made sad; and you have strengthened the hands of the wicked, so that he does not turn from his wicked way to save his life.
>
> Therefore you shall no longer envision futility nor practice divination; **for I will deliver My people out of your hand, and you shall know that I am the LORD.**"'"
> Ezekiel 13:20-23

How do we break the lies of the enemy and gain back the ground he has stolen from us? The answer is…Jesus – the Truth.

> "Jesus said to him, "I am the way, **the truth**, and the life. No one comes to the Father except through Me."
> John 14:6

Taken from "Refresh" by Sue Boldt

25

Helpful Verses...

Then Jesus said to those Jews who believed Him, "If you abide in My word, you are My disciples indeed. And you shall know the truth, and the truth shall make you free."
John 8:31-32

And a slave does not abide in the house forever, but a son abides forever. Therefore if the Son makes you free, you shall be free indeed.
John 8:35-36

Search me, O God, and know my heart;
Try me, and know my anxieties;
And see if there is any wicked way in me,
And lead me in the way everlasting."
Psalm 139:23-24

Behold, You desire truth in the inward parts,
And in the hidden part You will make me to know wisdom.
Psalm 51:6

Nevertheless when one turns to the Lord,
the veil is taken away.
Now the Lord is the Spirit;
and where the Spirit of the Lord is, there is liberty.
But we all, with unveiled face,
beholding as in a mirror the glory of the Lord,
are being transformed into the same image
from glory to glory, just as by the Spirit of the Lord.
 2 Corinthians 3:16-18

Likewise the Spirit also helps in our weaknesses...
Now He who searches the hearts
knows what the mind of the Spirit is,
because He makes intercession for the saints
according to the will of God.
And we know that all things work together for good
to those who love God,
to those who are the called according to His purpose.
Romans 8:26-28

He has delivered us from the power of darkness
and conveyed us into the kingdom of the Son of His love,
In whom we have redemption through His blood,
the forgiveness of sins.
Colossians 1:13-14

Possible Entry Points

_____

_____

_____

_____

_____

_____

_____

_____

_____

_____

_____

_____

_____

_____

_____

_____

_____

_____

- Occult Practices
- Sexual Abuse/Harm
- Alcoholism
- Drug Addiction
- Control
- Chaos
- Rage
- Violence
- Abandonment / Neglect
- Emotional abuse
- Unhealthy Media Exposure
- Verbal abuse
- Generational Bondages
- Fantasy
- Death in Family
- Divorce in Family
- Family Dysfunction
- Family Depression
- Generational Illnesses
- Curses
- Trauma
- Fearful Event
- Self-Harm
- Self-Indulgence
- Narcissism
- Any religion that doesn't proclaim Jesus as Lord, God, or the only way to salvation

Life Mapping

Positive Memories

0   7

Not So Positive Memories

Life Mapping

Positive Memories

14

Emotional Pain Words

- Abandoned
- Afraid
- Alone
- Angry
- Anxious
- Apathetic
- Ashamed
- Belittled
- Betrayed
- Confused
- Controlled
- Dirty
- Disappointed
- Disgusted
- Disrespected
- Embarrassed
- Empty
- Exposed
- Failure
- Fear
- Foolish
- Frustrated
- Hate
- Helpless
- Humiliated
- Hurt
- Inadequate
- Inferior
- Insecure

- Insignificant
- Left Out
- Lied to
- Lonely
- Lost
- Manipulated
- Mistreated
- Misunderstood
- Molested
- Neglected
- No Good
- Not Cherished
- Not heard
- Not valued
- Out of Control
- Overwhelmed
- Pathetic
- Performance
- Pressured
- Rejected
- Ruined
- Sad
- Scared
- Shame
- Stress
- Stupid
- Suffocated
- Suicidal
- Taken Advantage of

- Thwarted
- Trapped
- Trashy
- Ugly
- Unable to _____
- Unaccepted
- Unchosen
- Unclean
- Unfairly _____
- Unfit
- Unnecessary
- Unloved
- Unsafe
- Unwanted
- Used
- Violated
- Vulnerable
- Wasted
- Wicked
- Worthless
- Wounded

Possible Lies or Strongholds

- I am unworthy
- I am not significant
- I will be abandoned
- I am a victim and I always will be
- I am or will be rejected
- I am not beautiful or handsome
- I am not desirable
- I am rejected
- I am not deserving
- I out of control
- I am ashamed or shameful
- I will always be _____
- I am alone
- I am not enough
- I am too much
- I am overlooked
- I am guilty
- It's all up to me
- I need this _____ to bring me happiness
- I must protect myself
- I must provide for myself
- I am confused
- I have no future
- I must be in control
- I will always be fearful
- I cannot be forgiven
- I am hopeless or helpless
- I do not have a voice
- Abandonment
- Anger

- Any Addiction
- Co-Dependent
- Comparison
- Control
- Depression
- Divination – Preoccupation with the future
- Death – Preoccupation with
- Fear
- Gluttony
- Infirmity – Physical Illness
- Lust (All types)
- Martyr Mentality
- Performance Driven
- Perversion
- Pride
- Rebellion
- Religion – Legalism/Pseudo Spirituality
- Self-Absorption
- Self-Depravation
- Self-Hatred
- Self-Pity
- Sexual Perversion
- Shame
- Suicide
- Unforgiveness
- Vanity
- Victim Mentality
- Witchcraft or Idol Worship

Lies I Have Believed

Jesus' Truth to Me...

Lies I Have Believed

Jesus' Truth to Me...

My Journal ~ Week #1

Day #1

Day #2

Day #3

Day #4

Day #5

Day #6

Day #7

My Journal ~ Week #2

Day #1

Day #2

Day #3

Day #4

Day #5

Day #6

Day #7

My Journal ~ Week #3

Day #1

Day #2

Day #3

Day #4

Day #5

Day #6

Day #7

My Journal ~ Week #4

Day #1

Day #2

Day #3

Day #4

Day #5

Day #6

Day #7

My Journal ~ Week #5

Day #1

Day #2

Day #3

Day #4

Day #5

Day #6

Day #7

My Journal ~ Week #6

Day #1

Day #2

Day #3

Day #4

Day #5

Day #6

Day #7

My Journal

My Journal

My Journal

My Journal

My Journal

My Journal

My Journal

Resources

- Joyce Meyer, *Battlefield of the Mind*

- Neil Anderson, *The Bondage Breaker*

- Edward M. Smith, *Healing Life's Hurts*

- Debbie Alsdorf, Joan Edwards Kay, MA LMFT *It's Momplicated*

- Beth Moore, *Praying God's Word*

- Beth Moore, *Breaking Free*

- Dr. Carolyn Leaf, *Switch On Your Brain*

- Dr. Carolyn Leaf, *The 21-Day Brain Detox*, www.drleaf.com

- Jack Hayford, *Rebuilding the Real You*

- Jack Hayford, *Penetrating the Darkness*

- Dr. Daniel Brown, *Embracing Grace*

- Chris Hayward, *God's Cleansing Stream*

- John Eldredge, *Waking the Dead*

- John and Staci Eldredge, *Captivating*

- Henry Cloud, John Townsend, *Boundaries*

- Henry Cloud, John Townsend, *Changes that Heal*

- Jimmy Evans, Ann Billington, *Freedom From Your Past*

- Sue Boldt, *Refresh*

- Sue Boldt, *CrossPointe #1, #2, #3*

- Derek Prince, *They Shall Expel Demons*

- Marilyn Hontz, *Shame Lifter*

- Lysa TerKeurst, *Uninvited*

- Mike Mason, *Champagne for the Soul*

- *The New Spirit Filled Life Bible,* Jack W. Hayford , Executive Editor

- *Key Word Study Bible,* Spiro Zodhiates, Executive Editor

Made in the USA
Las Vegas, NV
07 February 2022